Assumption School
2310 East 7th Ave.
Hibbing, MN 55746

GRIN AND BEAR IT!

Make Me Laugh!

GRIN AND BEAR IT!
jokes about teddy bears

by Sharon Friedman & Irene Shere
pictures by Joan Hanson

Lerner Publications Company · Minneapolis

To the students and staff at Jackson Road Elementary School, Silver Spring, Maryland, whose wild enthusiasm for teddy bear riddles was the bear-y *inspiration for this book!*

Copyright © 1986 by Lerner Publications Company

All rights reserved. International copyright secured.
No part of this book may be reproduced in any form whatsoever
without permission in writing from the publisher except for
the inclusion of brief quotations in an acknowledged review.

Library of Congress Cataloging-in-Publication Data

Friedman, Sharon.
  Grin and bear it!

  (Make me laugh!)
  Summary: A collection of jokes about teddy bears including "What's the best way to catch a teddy bear robber? With a bear-glar alarm."
  1. Riddles, Juvenile. 2. Teddy bears—Anecdotes, facetiae, satire, etc. 3. Puns and punning. [1. Teddy bears—Wit and humor. 2. Riddles. 3. Wit and humor]
I. Shere, Irene. II. Hanson, Joan, ill. III. Title.
IV. Series.
PN6371.5.F754   1986   818'.5402   85-23903
ISBN 0-8225-0985-7 (lib. bdg.)

Manufactured in the United States of America

3 4 5 6 7 8 9 10 94 93 92 91 90 89

Q: What does a teddy bear say on a cold winter night?
A: Bearrrr (brrrr).

Q: What's a teddy bear's favorite nursery rhyme?
A: "Here We Go Round the Mul-bear-ry Bush."

Q: How did Baby Teddy Bear feel when Mother Teddy Bear left on a trip?
A: Un-bear-ably sad.

Q: What did Teddy Bear's friends say to him after he had blown out the candles on his cake?
A: Happy Bear-thday!

Q: How does one teddy bear say good-bye to another teddy bear?
A: With a bear hug.

Q: What did the teddy bear ride in when she went over Niagara Falls?
A: A bear-rel.

Q: What does a teddy bear eat when he's in Mexico?
A: Bear-ritos (burritos).

Q: Where did the teddy bears go to snorkle?
A: The Great Bear-rier Reef.

Q: What's Teddy Bear's favorite old-fashioned dessert?
A: Blue-bear-ry cobbler.

Q: What does Teddy Bear yell when he cuts down a tree?
A: Tim-bear!

Q: What famous teddy bear was born in a log cabin and became president of the United States?
A: A-bear-ham Lincoln.

Q: How do American Indian teddy bears ride their horses?
A: Bear-back.

Q: What famous statue welcomes teddy bear immigrants to the United States?
A: The Statue of Li-bear-ty.

Q: How does a teddy bear wade through a creek?
A: Bear-foot.

Q: What's Teddy Bear's favorite frozen ice?
A: Ras-bear-ry sher-bear-t.

Q: At what events do teddy bears grill hotdogs?
A: Bear-beques.

Q: What ferocious fish did the teddy bears see when they were snorkling?
A: A bear-racuda.

Q: What's the name of a famous World War I teddy bear?
A: The Red Bear-on.

Q: Where does the Russian teddy bear spend long, cold winters?
A: Si-bear-ia.

Q: Where in Canada does Sargeant Teddy Bear of the Mounties live?
A: Al-bear-ta.

Q: What kind of hat did the French teddy bear wear?
A: A bear-et (beret).

Q: What farm equipment does Farmer Teddy Bear use to carry rocks?
A: Wheel-bear-row.

Q: What's the best way to catch a teddy bear robber?
A: With a bear-glar alarm.

Q: What do you call a teddy bear fib?
A: A bear-faced lie.

Q: Why was Teddy Bear's face red?
A: Because he was em-bear-assed.

Q: What does Teddy Bear do on a bad day?
A: Grin and bear it.

Q: What green vegetable do teddy bears like in their salads?
A: Cucum-bear.

Q: What's Teddy Bear's favorite soda?
A: Root bear.

Q: What do teddy bears eat for breakfast?
A: Bear-an (bran) flakes.

Q: What do teddy bears spread on their toast?
A: Black-bear-ry jam.

Q: What food does Teddy Bear grill with his hotdogs?
A: Ham-bear-gers.

Q: Who holds the flag in the Teddy Bear Dress Parade?
A: The flag bear-er.

Q: What kind of voice does Papa Teddy Bear have?
A: Bear-i-tone.

Q: What's Teddy Bear's favorite kind of dancing?
A: Bear-eak dancing.

Q: What's Teddy Bear's favorite rhythm instrument?
A: Tam-bear-ine.

Q: How does Farmer Teddy Bear lift rocks to put them in a wheelbarrow?
A: Bear-handed.

Q: Where did Teddy Bear live when he was in the army?
A: Bear-racks.

Q: What did Mr. and Mrs. Teddy Bear take on their camping trip?
A: The bear necessities.

Q: What's Teddy Bear's favorite fruit?
A: Straw-bear-ries.

Q: What screeched when Teddy Bear's car came to a stop?
A: Bear-akes.

Q: What's Teddy Bear's favorite dinosaur?
A: Bear-ontosaurus.

Q: What road block stopped visitors from entering the teddy bear army camp?
A: A bear-ricade.

Q: Where do teddy bears go to get books?
A: The li-bear-y.

Q: What does Teddy Bear wear to keep her hair out of her eyes?
A: Bear-ettes.

Q: Where was the smoke coming from on Teddy Bear's car?
A: The car-bear-ator.

Q: What meal does Teddy Bear eat when he sleeps through breakfast?
A: Bear-runch (brunch).

Q: What kind of dog rescued the teddy bear when he was stranded in the Alps?
A: A St. Bear-nard.

Q: What does Teddy Bear do during the winter months?
A: Hi-bear-nate.

Q: What famous British teddy bear wrote *Romeo and Juliet*?
A: William Shakes-bear.

Q: What do teddy bears take for a bad headache?
A: As-bear-in (aspirin).

Q: What did the teddy bear call the story of her life?
A: Her auto-bear-ography.

Q: How did the teddy bear get through this book?
A: Just bear-ly.

ABOUT THE ARTIST

JOAN HANSON lives with her husband and two sons in Afton, Minnesota. Her distinctive, deliberately whimsical pen-and-ink drawings have illustrated more than 30 children's books. Ms. Hanson is also an accomplished weaver. A graduate of Carleton College, Hanson enjoys tennis, skiing, sailing, reading, traveling, and walking in the woods surrounding her home.

ABOUT THE AUTHORS

SHARON FRIEDMAN lives in Silver Spring, Maryland, with her husband, Stephen, and their two sons, Robbie and Lee. She was a third grade teacher for eight years and is currently the president of her sons' PTA. Sharon enjoys tennis, dancing, and puppetry, and presents puppet shows and puppet-making workshops at area schools.

IRENE SHERE had the expert help of her children, Holly and Brett, when creating and testing these riddles. She enjoys being with children—both as a teacher and as a mother and active school volunteer. Irene spends her free moments drawing, ice skating, and playing with computers. She lives with her husband, Steve, and their children in a glass house surrounded by trees in Silver Spring, Maryland.

Make Me Laugh!

CAN YOU MATCH THIS?
CAT'S OUT OF THE BAG!
CLOWNING AROUND!
DUMB CLUCKS!
ELEPHANTS NEVER FORGET!
FACE THE MUSIC!
FOSSIL FOLLIES!
GO HOG WILD!
GOING BUGGY!
GRIN AND BEAR IT!
HAIL TO THE CHIEF!
IN THE DOGHOUSE!
KISS A FROG!
LET'S CELEBRATE!
OUT TO LUNCH!
OUT TO PASTURE!
SNAKES ALIVE!
SOMETHING'S FISHY!
SPACE OUT!
STICK OUT YOUR TONGUE!
WHAT A HAM!
WHAT'S YOUR NAME?
WHAT'S YOUR NAME, AGAIN?
101 ANIMAL JOKES
101 FAMILY JOKES
101 KNOCK-KNOCK JOKES
101 MONSTER JOKES
101 SCHOOL JOKES
101 SPORTS JOKES

DATE DUE

NOV 22	MAY 07 Ⓚ	
DEC 06 2		
JAN 03	DEC 12 K	
JAN. 3 13	MR. 18 ①	
MAR 07 ②	APR 2 2	
APR. 1 8 1	②	
MAY 2 ①	FEB 7 1996 1	
MAY 9 ①	JAN 25 2000 ∅	
SEP. 1 9 ③	3A	
OCT 3	JAN 10 2002 4B	
OCT 17 Ⓚ	SEP 2005 ④	
NOV 27	APR 28 2010	
JAN 7 ④		
JAN ①		
FEB. 13 K		
MAR. 06 K		
APR 10 ①		
Ⓚ		
JAN 5 2000 261-2500		Printed in USA